# CHRISTIAN CROSS STITCH

## GISELA BANBURY

SEARCH PRESS

First published in Great Britain 1999

Search Press Limited
Wellwood, North Farm Road,
Tunbridge Wells, Kent TN2 3DR

Text copyright © Gisela Banbury 1999

Photographs by Search Press Studios
Photographs and design copyright © Search Press Ltd. 1999

ISBN 0 85532 839 8

**Suppliers**
If you have any difficulty in obtaining any of the materials and
equipment mentioned in this book, then please write to the
publishers at the address above, for a current list of stockists,
which includes firms who operate a mail-order service.

**Publisher's note**
The step-by-step photographs in this book feature the author,
Gisela Banbury. No models have been used. All designs in this
book were created by the author, apart from the christening
gown on page 32 which was designed by Angela Dewar. All
finished embroideries were worked by the author unless stated
otherwise.

*Page 1*
*This small panel of the eagle (part of the chart on page 31)*
*was worked by Angela Dewar. It is embroidered on 11*
*count, red Aida cloth using three strands of cotton in gold,*
*orange, yellows and browns. When used on its own, the eagle*
*is regarded as the symbol of the Resurrection, based on the*
*early belief that the eagle periodically renewed its plumage*
*and its youth: Psalm 103, verse 5, 'Thy youth is renewed like*
*the eagles'.*

*Page 3*
*Bookmark featuring the peacock, a symbol of immortality, in*
*all its colourful glory. It was worked with three strands of*
*cotton on 14 count, red Aida cloth.*

Colour separation by P&W Graphics, Singapore
Printed in Spain by Elkar S. Coop. Bilbao 48012

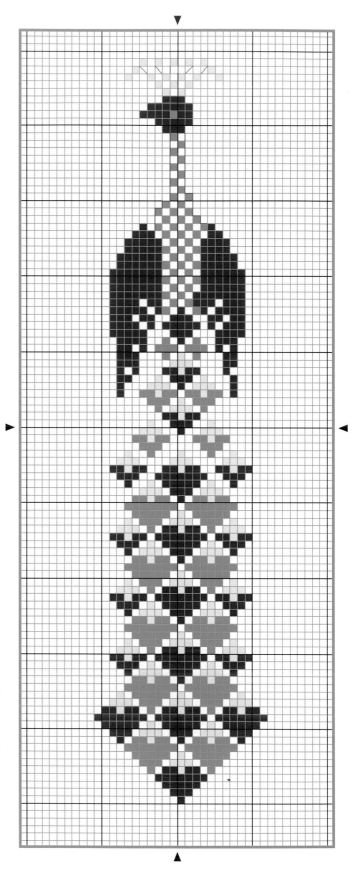

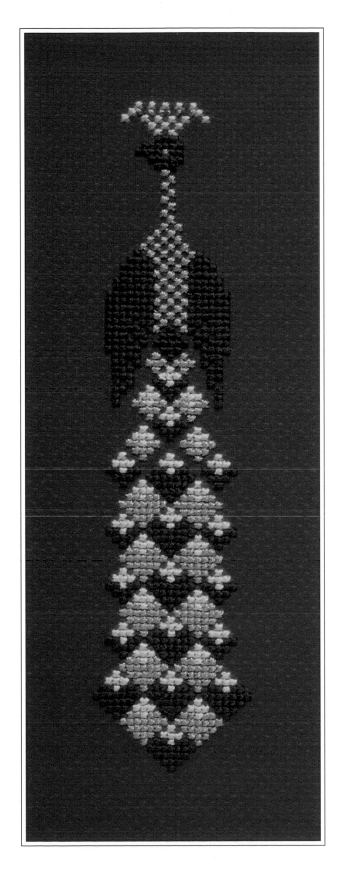

# CONTENTS

# INTRODUCTION

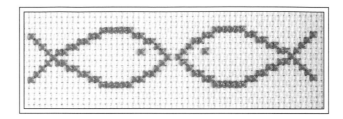

Since the early days of the Christian Church, especially in times of suppression and persecution, Christians have used symbols to communicate with each other. Probably the best known of these ancient symbols is the stylised fish, which is still visible in the catacombs of Rome, where it marked secret meeting places for Christians. The fish became the symbol of Christ because the initial letters of the five Greek words for *Jesus Christ, God's Son, Saviour* form the Greek word *IXOUS* which means fish.

From these early beginnings, these symbols have found their way into our daily lives through Christian arts. We use them as decorations in our churches and our homes, to remind us of our beliefs and to celebrate events in the Church calendar, as well as in our own lives. The stylised images are very suitable for embroidery designs and are perfect as patterns for cross stitch work.

A basic cross stitch consists of two straight stitches of equal length, lying diagonally across each other to occupy a square. These small units are the building blocks of all cross stitch designs, from small motifs to more complex pictures. The geometric character of the stitches also makes them very suitable for the creation of different scripts and numbers.

I have chosen well-known symbols from nature – flowers, trees, plants, animals, birds and fish, and different forms of the cross. These are used for various projects that include cards, book-marks, book covers, a box lid, a tray, a cushion cover, panels and samplers. The charts can be worked exactly as presented or you can combine parts of them to create a new design. Borders and text can be added as embellishment. Charts for motifs which only appear on samplers are included on pages 46 and 47. My aim is to encourage the novice, and to offer new ideas to embroiderers of all abilities.

*Opposite*
*An attractive sampler worked by Liz Cannon and Angelar Dewar. It includes symbols taken from the designs in this book: the lily is used as an attribute to the Virgin Mary; the dove with an olive branch stands for peace; pomegranates are often connected with the church family; red roses symbolise martyrdom; the fish is an abbreviation of 'Jesus Christ God's Son Saviour'; the lamb represents Christ, who was crucified for us; grapes and wheat are symbols of the sacraments. It also includes a few crosses and borders. When worked on 14 count Aida cloth or 28 count evenweave, the sampler measures 10 x 12¼in (25 x 31cm).*

# MATERIALS AND TOOLS

You do not require much to start cross stitch embroidery. A few embroidery threads and a piece of fabric, a suitable needle and a pair of scissors will be enough to start with.

## Threads

Threads may be made of cotton, linen, wool, silk, man-made fibres or even metal. They should preferably be smooth, to give a clean and crisp appearance to the embroidery. Stranded cottons are the most commonly used, but for more adventurous work you could try some of the novelty threads that are now available. The thickness of the threads should always complement the fabric you are using.

## Needles

Cross stitch is best worked with a tapestry needle. Its blunt point will ensure that each entry into the fabric is made into a hole and not through a warp or a weft thread of the fabric. The needle should have an eye big enough to take your working thread, and a shank slim enough to slip easily through the fabric.

Recommended needle sizes for Aida cloth:

| Aida | Needle size |
|------|-------------|
| 6 | 18 |
| 8 | 20 |
| 12 | 22 |
| 14 | 24 |
| 16 | 26 |
| 18 | 28 |

## Scissors

Embroidery threads should be cut with small, sharp scissors. If the tips are curved, like nail scissors, you are less likely to inadvertently cut into your fabric when trimming thread ends. You will also need a pair of dressmaker's scissors for cutting fabric. Keep your embroidery scissors separate – do not use them for anything else and they will stay sharp for a long time.

## Fabrics

Cross stitch is generally worked on an evenweave fabric, which has the same number of warp and weft threads to the square centimetre (inch). An evenweave fabric ensures that the stitches are square and all of the same size. Fabrics can be made of many different fibres, the most common being cotton, linen and viscose, or any mixture of these.

Most linens, and some cottons, have a plain weave, and, on these, cross stitch is usually worked over at least two threads.

Hardanger fabric may be made of linen or cotton, or a mixture of the two, and all the threads are arranged in pairs. Cross stitch is worked over at least two pairs.

Aida cloth is a fabric specially designed for cross stitch. During the weaving process the warp and weft threads are bundled into even groups and each cross stitch is worked over one group of threads.

Tapestry canvas is an evenweave fabric but, generally, it is not considered suitable for cross stitch. However, it can be used in many different ways for experimental work.

Waste canvas can be used as a grid to work a pattern on to a fabric that is too fine or densely woven to count the threads. It is woven as a double canvas with vertical blue lines at regular intervals.

*Opposite*
*Stranded embroidery cotton, the most popular yarn used for cross stitch, is available in a wide variety of shades and tones of colour, including gold and silver. A selection of different sizes of tapestry needles and a thimble make stitching easier. Embroidery scissors with curved blades lessen the chance of cutting into the fabric when trimming threads.*

The canvas is laid over the background fabric and the embroidery is worked over the canvas into the fabric. The canvas is then carefully removed, thread by thread, leaving the embroidery behind.

Non-woven fabrics such as plastic and paper can also be used as a surface for cross stitch. These are very suitable for children's work, as well as for more experimental pieces of embroidery.

## Frames

It is not always necessary to frame the fabric, and many of the projects shown in this book can be worked in the hand. However, an inexperienced embroiderer may find it easier to achieve an even tension by working with a frame. It is also easier to count the threads if the fabric is stretched in a frame. For softer fabrics, a tambour or a small machine embroidery frame is suitable. The frame does not have to encircle the whole design; it can be moved along as work progresses. For stiffer fabrics a slate frame is recommended.

## Optional equipment

Here are a few additional items that you may find useful.

A table lamp fitted with a 'daylight bulb' will help when choosing colours in artificial light.

A magnifier mounted on a stand helps avoid eye strain. Some magnifiers have a built-in light source and I find them a real pleasure to use.

See-through plastic bags are useful for organising your threads and they make it easier to find a particular colour. Store the bags in labelled shoe boxes.

Cardboard tubes from kitchen paper and food wrap are ideal for storing fabric, which should be rolled rather than folded.

You can also embellish your work with beads, sequins, thin metal foil and beautiful handmade papers, so start collecting now.

*A selection of fabrics and frames. A slate or tapestry frame is best for large projects, while round frames are suitable for small designs. Always use sharp scissors to cut the fabric.*

# GETTING STARTED

In this chapter I show you the stitches used for the projects in this book, the use of charts, how to choose and prepare the fabric, why you should separate strands of embroidery cotton and general sewing techniques.

## Stitches

The designs in this book are worked with just full cross stitch, three-quarter cross stitch and back stitch.

### Full cross stitch

Full cross stitch consists of two straight stitches of equal length, crossed diagonally so that each complete stitch occupies a square of fabric. To achieve a crisp, even appearance, make all the top stitches point in the same direction. Work each stitch as four separate journeys, and always finish one stitch before moving on to the next. When you have worked a few stitches, sew the tail end of the thread into the back of them, as shown on page 13.

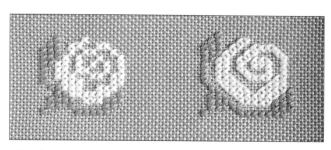

*The chart opposite (bottom left) was used as a guide for these two white roses. The rose on the left is worked in the traditional style using full cross stitches, and voiding is used to give the flower its shape. On the right, the rose is worked with full and three-quarter cross stitches – note how this style gives a more rounded and fuller shape.*

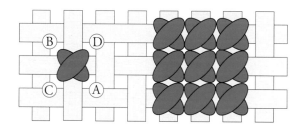

1. Bring the thread from the back of the fabric to the front at point A, leaving a 2in (5cm) tail on the underside.

2. Take the thread through to the back of the fabric at point B. Hold the tail at the back and do not pull the stitch too tight.

3. Bring the thread back up at point C.

4. Finally, take the thread down at point D to complete the stitch.

### Three-quarter cross stitch

Diagonal lines worked with full cross stitches are rather jagged. You can create a smooth diagonal line using a three-quarter cross stitch. The stitch is worked as shown in the diagram below: bring the thread up at A, down at B, up again at C and down at D. Note how you can change the angle of the stitch to turn a square into a reasonable circle.

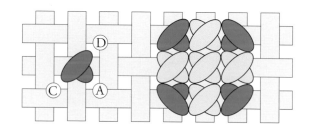

## Back stitch

Use this stitch to define detail and to create thin outlines. It can be worked in any direction but in this example the stitch is worked from right to left.

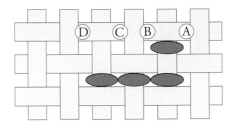

1. Bring the thread up at point B and back down at point A to complete the first stitch.

2. On the back of the fabric, move to the left, bring the thread up at point C and take it down at point B to make the second stitch.

3. Continue by coming up at D and down at C, and so on along the length of the design.

## Charts

Most of the charts in this book have a grey grid on a white ground. Each coloured square represents a stitch and each white one a space. However, when the design requires white stitches a coloured ground has been used. To make counting easier, every tenth line is drawn in black. The centre of the design is shown by small arrows and you should make your first stitch in the space closest to this point (see page 12).

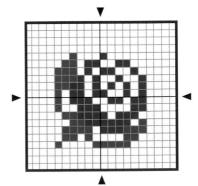

*Chart for red roses right, and the white ones opposite.*

## Choosing fabric

All evenweave fabrics are identified by their number of holes per inch (2.5cm) of fabric.

For example, a plain weave fabric with a count of 20 has twenty threads and twenty holes per inch (2.5cm). On such fabrics, cross stitches are worked over at least two threads to give ten stitches per inch (2.5cm) of fabric. A design with forty stitches across its width would therefore be 4in (10cm) wide.

To work the same design to the same size on Aida cloth you would need fabric with a count of 10, since the stitches are only worked over one group of threads.

To make the design smaller, without changing the number of stitches, choose a fabric with a larger count. Conversely, to make it bigger, choose a fabric with a smaller count.

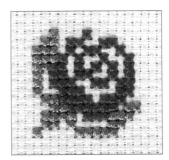

*14 count fabric (4 strands)*       *18 count fabric (2 strands)*

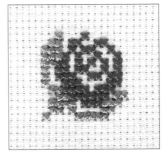

*18 count fabric (3 strands)*       *22 count fabric (1 strand)*

*These four roses have been worked from the same chart on fabrics of differing count numbers. The rose stays the same, but its size alters with the fabric count number – the smaller the count, the bigger the rose. You can also affect the look of the embroidery by varying the number of strands of embroidery cotton used. In general, the larger the fabric count number, the fewer strands of cotton should be used.*

# Preparing the fabric

First, secure all the raw edges of your fabric by oversewing, or they will get disturbed every time you pick up your embroidery and will begin to fray.

Next, to ensure that the finished embroidery is in the middle of the background, find the centre of the fabric and mark it with a pin. Match this point with the centre of the chart.

Finally, if you decide to use a frame, now is the time to frame up your fabric.

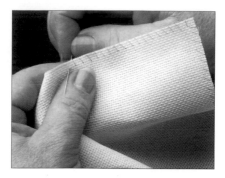

1. Use a strong thread to oversew the raw edges of the fabric. This will prevent fraying.

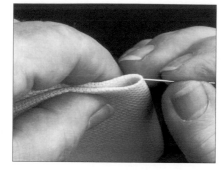

2. Fold the fabric in half vertically and then horizontally. Mark the centre of the fabric (where the two fold lines cross) with a pin.

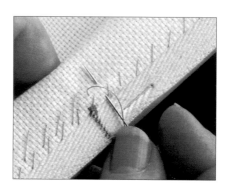

3. Secure the fabric to the frame following the manufacturer's instructions. Here I am fastening a piece of fabric to a slate frame, aligning the centre of the fabric with the centre of one of the rollers.

# Threading a needle

Stranded cotton consists of six strands. This is often too thick a yarn to work with – most designs can be worked with two, three or four strands. I find it best to separate a length of cotton thread into individual strands and then select the number strands I need. This practice will also ensure that the strands lay side by side and give neat even stitches. Stitches made with twisted strands can look rough and uneven.

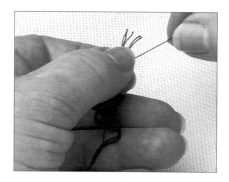

1. Cut a length of thread about 15in (40cm) long. Hold the end of the thread and then pull out individual strands, one by one.

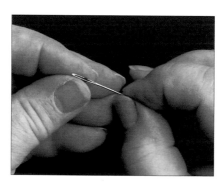

2. Bring the required number of strands together and, without twisting them, thread them on the needle.

# Sewing techniques

The appearance of your embroidery depends on the quality of your stitching. Do not split fabric threads – only stitch into holes. Try to keep all the stitches the same size, ensure that all top stitches point the same way, and work with a tension that does not distort the weave of the fabric. Follow these basic rules and your embroidery will have the appearance of a professionally-worked piece. When working your stitches, you may turn the embroidery upside down, but I suggest that you do not turn it sideways. Try it, and you should notice how it brakes your rhythm and, inevitably, you will start working the top stitch in the wrong direction.

**Note**

When working on a design that includes many colours, try not to thread the ends of dark coloured threads through the back of light-coloured stitches. The dark colours may shine through the fabric and 'grey' the appearance of the embroidery.

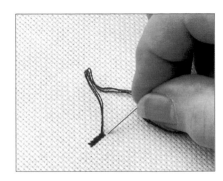

1. Insert the needle from the back of fabric. Pull the working thread through to the front leaving a tail, about 2in (5cm) long, at the back of the work. Hold this tail out of the way with one finger, while you work the first few stitches.

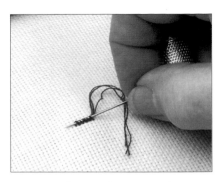

2. Turn the work over and use a second needle to secure the tail end through the back of the first stitches. Trim off the end.

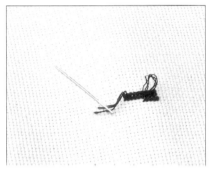

3. When the working thread starts to run out, take it through to the back of the work and sew it through the completed stitches.

4. When starting new threads, work them straight into the back of existing stitches.

## Pressing finished embroideries

When your embroidery is finished, lay it face down on a very soft surface, such as a folded blanket. Cover it with a clean, damp pressing cloth and iron it gently with a medium hot iron.

# FLOWERS AND FRUIT

In the Gospel we are used to hearing Christ speak in parables. For instance, in *John 15:5*, Jesus compares himself to a vine and us to its branches, to show symbolically that we can do nothing without him. Later, we see artists making use of plants as symbols in the same way – to add deeper meaning to their paintings and to give hidden messages only understood by the informed. On the following pages, I show designs using symbolic fruit and flowers.

15

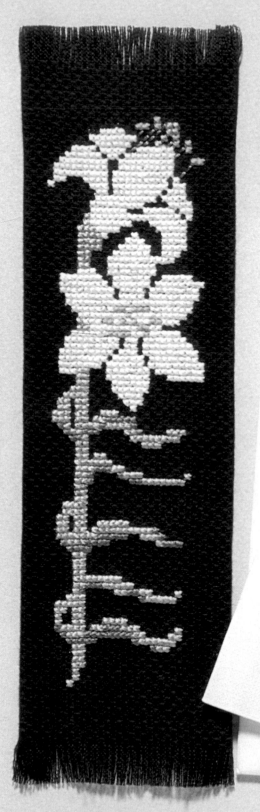

# Lily

*The lily, with its brilliant white colour, symbolises purity. In Christian art it has often been used in connection with the Virgin Mary, but it is also attributed to a number of saints as a symbol for chastity. When shown as a fleur-de-lys it symbolises royalty.*

*Lise Hawkins used the lily chart opposite to create this bookmark and card.*

## Card

The colouring and shape of the lily makes it a striking subject for embroidery and, with its high and virtuous connections, it is a suitable motif to use on gifts or small tokens. A handmade card gives a double pleasure – to the sender, who enjoys making it, and to the recipient.

This is an ideal project for the beginner. Very few materials are needed and the work does not take long to complete. Pre-cut and folded cards are available in many different shapes and sizes from craft or art shops, and the finished embroidery is easily inserted.

*You will need*

Pre-cut card with a 4¼ x 3¼in (10.5 x 8cm) oval opening

14 count, Aida cloth, slightly smaller than the size of the card

Tapestry needle No. 24

Stranded cotton: white, light and dark yellow, and light and dark green

Fabric glue or double-sided sticky tape

The card is worked using four strands of cotton. Prepare the fabric and start stitching (see pages 12 and 13), following the chart from the centre outwards. The horizontal centre for the card is shown by the upper pair of arrows.

When the embroidery is finished, press it lightly (see page 13). If necessary, trim the fabric to size, so that it fits easily into the pre-cut card. Make sure the design is well centred and straight. Apply fabric glue or pieces of double-sided tape around the aperture of the card and carefully place the fabric in position.

## Bookmark

The bookmark requires a 10 x 3½in (25 x 9cm) piece of 14 count Aida cloth. Work the complete chart: flower head, stalk and leaves. Trim the fabric to within 10 holes of the embroidery all round. On the sides, fold half of this allowance to the back of the bookmark and secure it with plain over-sewing or a row of cross stitch in self-coloured sewing cotton or embroidery cotton. At the top and bottom edges, withdraw the weft threads from the fabric to create a fringe.

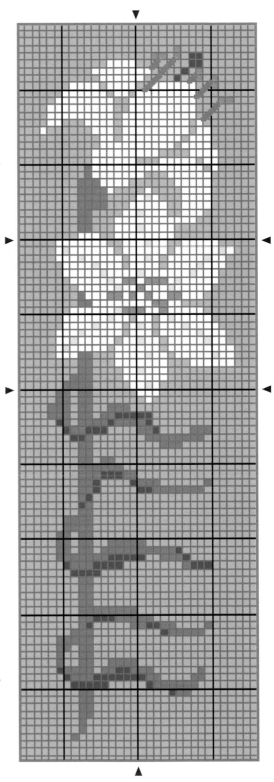

# Tree of Knowledge

*In Genesis 2:9 we read that two trees stood in the middle of the Garden of Eden, one of which was the Tree of Knowledge of Good and Evil. It features in many paintings of Adam and Eve in paradise and is usually shown as an apple tree.*

## Book cover

The Tree of Knowledge is a very suitable subject for a book cover, and the oblong shape of a tree fits well on many books.

The measurements given in the following instructions are for a 5½ x 7½in (14 x 19cm) book with a 1in (2.5cm) spine.

---

*You will need*

14 count, Aida cloth, 20 x 8½in (50 x 21.5cm)

Lining fabric, the same size as the Aida cloth

Stranded cotton: light and dark green, light and dark brown, yellow, orange and red

Sewing needle and cotton to match the colour of your fabric

Tapestry needle No. 24

---

Oversew the raw edges of the fabric to stop it fraying.

Find the centre of the fabric as described on page 12 and mark it with a pin. Now measure 3in (7.5cm) to the right of this point and mark the centre point of the front cover design.

*Continued overleaf*

*Opposite*
*The Tree of Knowledge book cover worked on oatmeal, 14 count Aida cloth.*

This is rather a large piece so I suggest that it is worked in a slate frame. Work the design using three strands of cotton throughout. Press the finished embroidery as described on page 13.

Lay the Aida cloth face down on the right side of the lining fabric. Using a seam allowance of ½in (1.25cm), hand- or machine-stitch round all four sides of the fabric, leaving a 2in (5cm) opening. Trim the corners and turn the work right side out through the opening in the seam. From the wrong side press the fabric gently into shape, using a damp pressing cloth. Close the opening with invisible hand stitching.

Fit the cover around the closed book and fold the side flaps to the inside to determine the fold line. Join the top and bottom edges of the flaps to the cover using slip stitch.

**Calculations for other sizes of books**

1. Measure the height of the spine of the book and add 1in (2.5cm) for seam-allowance.

2. Measure the closed book from the front cover edge, round the spine, to the back cover edge. Add another two-thirds of this measurement for flaps and seam allowance.

3. Cut the fabric and lining to the measurements taken in steps 1 and 2.

4. Mark the centre of the fabric (see page 12).

5. Measure the width of the spine, add the width of the cover and divide the total by two.

6. Move the distance calculated in step 5 horizontally to the right of the centre of the fabric and mark the centre of the design.

# Pomegranate

*The pomegranate, with its many seeds organised in neat rows, is often connected with the Church family, where many different people are united to form a whole. Because of the quantity of seeds inside one fruit, it also stands for fertility and for the hope of immortality. Since it is not the fruit itself, but the many seeds inside that are symbolic, the pomegranate is usually shown split or sliced open to reveal the seeds.*

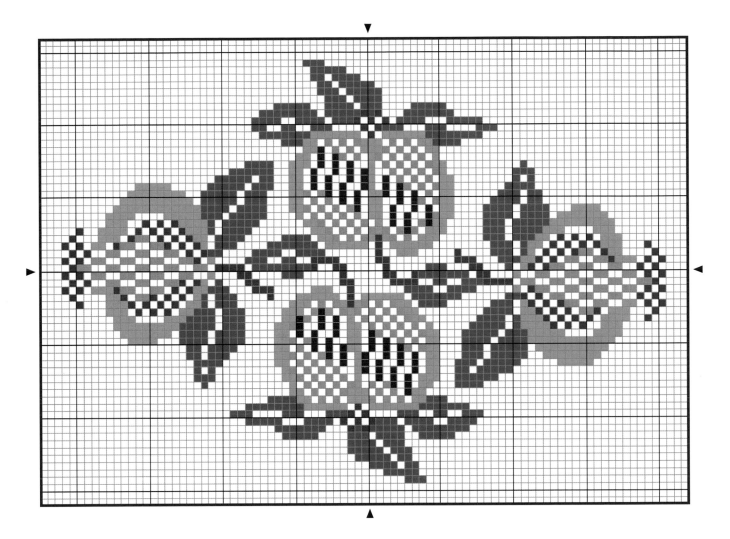

## Tray insert

The design for the inset of this wooden tray shows pomegranates sliced open in two different ways. The fruit has been arranged to fill the central oval opening of a tray.

*You will need*

Wooden tray, approximately 12 x 10in (30 x 25cm), with an oval opening

14 count, Aida cloth, slightly smaller than the dimensions of the tray

Stranded cotton: green, beige, light red and dark red

Tapestry needle No. 24

Sewing cotton and needle for oversewing

Oversew the raw edges of your fabric and mark the centre as described on page 12. This design may be worked in a round or Tambour frame which should be at least the same size as the opening of the tray. Work the design, from the centre outwards, using three strands of cotton.

When the embroidery is finished, press it as described on page 13 and insert it into the tray following the manufacturer's instructions.

# Vine and wheat

*Although Christ used the vine as a symbol for himself, the combination of vine and wheat represents the wine and bread of the Eucharist.*

### Bread basket cloth

For this project, I combined a border of wheat ears, bunches of grapes and vine leaves, with a square corner design that incorporates a challis and Host.

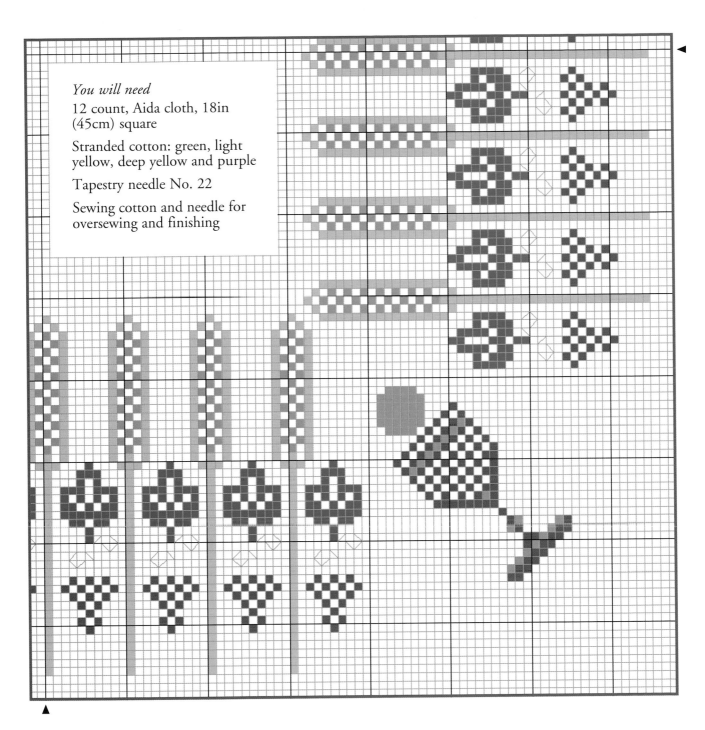

**You will need**

12 count, Aida cloth, 18in (45cm) square

Stranded cotton: green, light yellow, deep yellow and purple

Tapestry needle No. 22

Sewing cotton and needle for oversewing and finishing

Oversew the raw edges of your fabric and mark the centre of one side.

Use all six strands of light yellow cotton to work the stem of wheat in the centre of the border. The first stitch at the base of the stem should be placed eighteen holes in from the edge of the fabric. Work all seven ears of wheat. The first ear of wheat on the second side is best started from the top, where it is only one stitch distant from the last wheat of the previous side. When the design is finished, press the cloth as described on page 13.

To form a hem, fold over the first four bundles of threads, then the next six bundles and hemstitch by hand or machine. Mitre the corners.

23

# ANIMALS AND BIRDS

In pre-Christian Egypt, birds were used to depict the spiritual world. In Christian art, birds in general are used to represent winged souls.

Animals are often used as symbols for sacrifice, patience and hope, or as attributes to saints. No Nativity scene is complete without an ox and an ass. We are also very familiar with the picture of a lamb representing Christ, and a dove with an olive branch symbolising peace. In the following chapter you will find cross stitch designs for peacocks, doves and the symbols for the Evangelists.

25

# Peacock

The peacock design shown on page 3 is repeated here in 'Assisi' work, using one colour only. From the ancient belief that its flesh never decayed, the peacock became a Christian symbol of immortality and of the Resurrection. It is with this meaning that it features in scenes of the Nativity. The beauty of the 'hundred eyes' in the peacock's tail may also have something to do with its popularity with artists. These 'eyes' are said to represent the 'all seeing' Church.

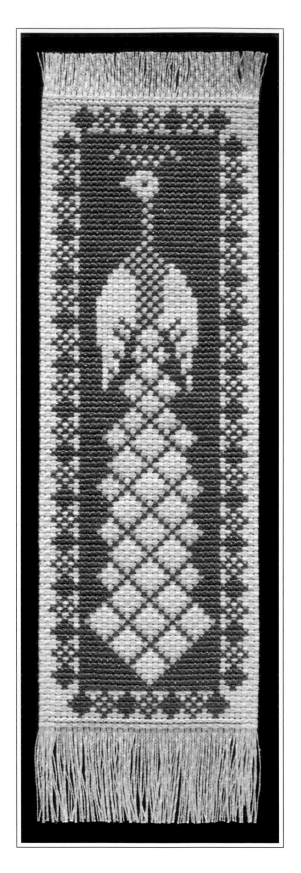

*This bookmark, worked by Nina Mills, is embroidered as Assisi work, a variation of traditional cross stitch embroidery that is said to have originated in Assisi, northern Italy. The same stitches are used – cross stitch as the filling stitch, and back stitch or, more often Holbein stitch, to outline the design if this is felt necessary. Assisi work appears as a 'negative' of ordinary cross stitch embroidery in that it is the background that is stitched and the motive, in this case the peacock, that is left free. The colour scheme is always simple, often employing only one colour, red or blue. Sometimes two tones of one colour may be used. Because of its dignified appearance, it is often used for ecclesiastical or heraldic work.*

## Bookmark

This chart is an Assisi work variation of the colourful peacock shown on pages 2–3, with the addition of a simple border.

---

*You will need*

14 count, light coloured Aida cloth, 3½ x 10in (9 x 25cm)

Stranded cotton: blue

Tapestry needle No. 24

Sewing cotton and needle for oversewing and finishing

---

Oversew the raw edges and find the centre of the fabric as described on page 12. Work the design from the centre outwards, using two strands of cotton throughout.

Work a row of cross stitches in self-coloured sewing cotton close to the top and bottom edge of the embroidery. Fringe out the rest of the fabric by withdrawing the weft threads.

Fold over the seam allowance along the two long sides of the bookmark. Work rows of cross stitch close to the embroidered border, using self-coloured sewing cotton and stitching through both layers of fabric. Trim off the surplus fabric on the back.

Press the finished embroidery as described on page 13.

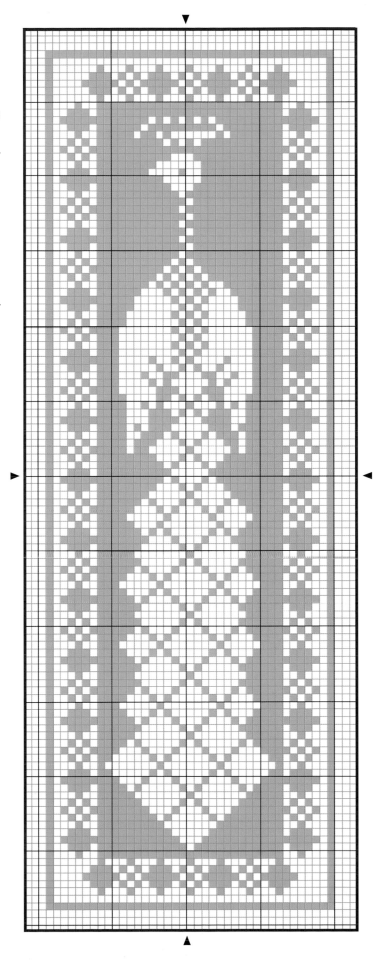

## Cushion cover

A peacock with his beautiful tail feathers fully displayed produces a circular pattern that is very suitable for decorating cushion covers.

*You will need*

Cushion pad, 16 x 16in (40 x 40cm)

14 count, blue Aida cloth, 16in (40cm) square, with rounded corners. (Use a cup or a glass to shape the corners)

Fabric of your choice for the back of the cushion, the same size and shape as the Aida cloth.

Stranded cotton: blue, green, yellow, copper, black, and a short length of dark yellow for outlines of the beak and eye

Tapestry needle No. 24

Thick piping cord, 65in (165cm) long

Bias binding in a compatible colour, 150in (4m) long and 2in (5cm) wide (depending on the thickness of your piping cord)

Zip, 14in (35cm) long

Sewing cotton to match fabrics, sewing needle or sewing machine and dressmaker's pins.

*This cushion, worked by Phyliss Baines, is embroidered on blue, 14 count Aida cloth. The piping is peacock green and the cushion is backed with a light blue furnishing fabric.*

Oversew the raw edges of your fabric and find its centre as shown on page 12. Embroider the design from the centre outward using two strands of cotton. When the embroidery is finished, press it gently as described on page 13.

Cover the piping cord with bias strip, gathering the strip to give a ruffled effect. Attach the cord to the embroidered cover, starting and finishing at the centre of the bottom edge. Join the two ends by trimming the cord to size and joining the bias strip.

Attach the zip to one side of the back of the cushion, either by hand or with the zipper foot of your sewing machine. Place the front and back of the cushion, right sides together, and match all edges, the bottom one of which will be formed by the zip. Open 2in (5cm) of the zip. Stitch all the way round the edge, as close as possible to the piping cord inside the two layers of fabric. Neaten the

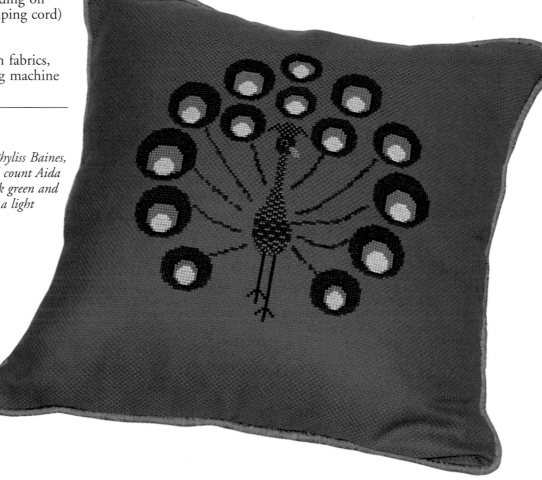

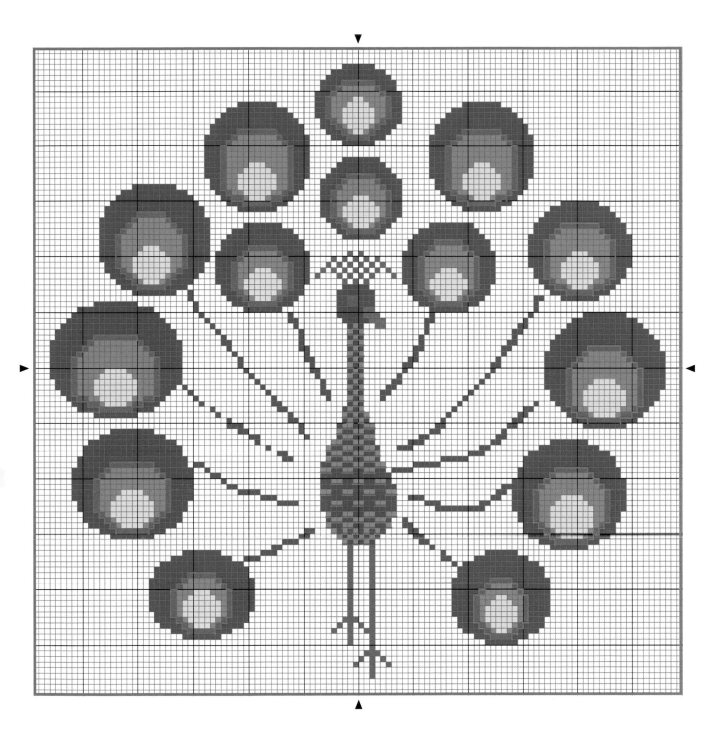

edges, open the zip further and turn the cushion cover right side out. Place the cushion pad inside the cover, stuff it well into the corners and close the zip.

If you have no experience of using piping and zip fasteners, you can simplify the make up of the cushion. Lay the two pieces of material right sides together and machine round three sides. Neaten the edges and turn the cover right side out. Place the cushion pad inside, tucking it well into the corners, and then use slip stitch to close the last side by hand.

# The Four Evangelists

*Many churches have paintings of the Four Evangelists, not represented as actual portraits, but as symbolic winged creatures: Matthew, a man; Mark, a lion; Luke, an ox; and John, an eagle. The source of this convention was a passage from* Ezekiel 1:5–14, *where the Prophet tells of a strange vision of the four beasts. In* Apocalypse 3, *we read about similar creatures surrounding the throne of God, hence they are known as the apocalyptic beasts.*

**Four Evangelists panel**

This design has enough content to be used as a mounted and framed panel. It would also make a very handsome cover for the New Testament, as a gift to a confirmation candidate.

*You will need*

14 count, blue Aida cloth, 16in (40cm) square

Stranded cotton: dark blue, gold, dark, medium and light brown, dark, medium and light yellow, and short lengths of green, pink, white and dark grey.

Tapestry needle No. 24

Sewing cotton and needle for oversewing and finishing

Oversew the raw edges, find the centre of your fabric as described on page 12 and frame it up.

Start the embroidery in the centre and work outwards, using two strands of cotton. Work the halos in different shades of yellow, some with one strand of yellow combined with one strand of gold. The 'eyes' in the wings are worked with one strand of light yellow combined with one strand of gold.

Press the finished embroidery as described on page 13 and mount it in a suitable picture frame.

*The four parts of this design will also stand by themselves as shown on page 1, where the eagle is worked as a single unit. To enlarge the designs, use the charts as given, but work on a fabric with a smaller count number.*

# Dove

*In Christian symbolism, the dove represents the Holy Spirit. This comes from the words of John the Baptist, ' I saw the spirit coming down from heaven like a dove and resting upon him'.*

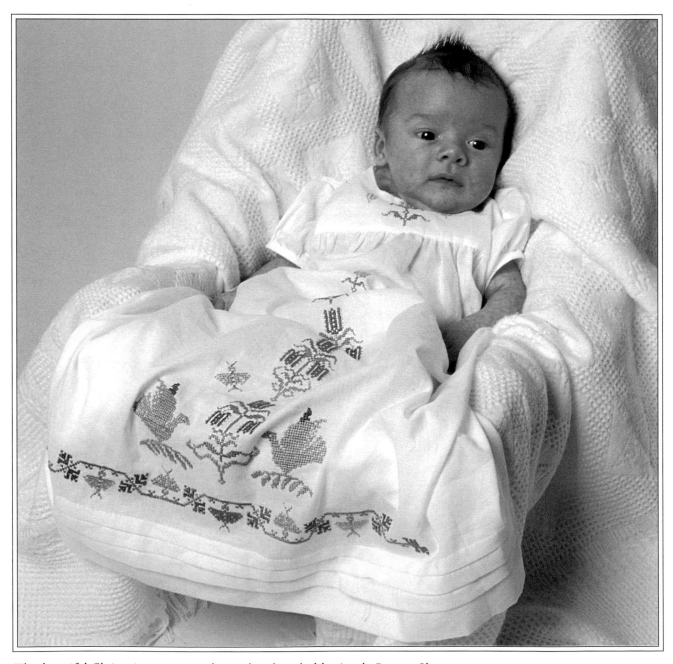

*This beautiful Christening gown was designed and worked by Angela Dewar. She used a commercial dress pattern, but sewed the entire gown by hand.*

## Christening gown

The dove appears in paintings of the baptism of Christ, so it is a very suitable symbol to be embroidered on to Christening gowns for infant baptisms. The butterfly, as a symbol of hope, is equally suitable and the pattern for this gown features both symbols.

The pattern is designed to fit the size of gown given on page 34, but you can spread the design out, or eliminate some of the elements, according to the available space. You can buy ready-made gowns or you can make one from a commercial pattern.

*The design for the yoke. The chart is shown on page 34.*

*The design for the skirt. It is symmetrical about the centre line, and segmented charts are shown on page 35.*

*The butterfly motifs are designed to be embroidered on the bias, and the chart is shown on page 35.*

*The border design for the hem. It is symmetrical about the centre line and its chart is shown on page 34.*

The pattern for the skirt design can be worked as a whole, except for the two butterflies above the doves which are placed on the bias, on a triangular piece of waste canvas, 15in (38cm) across the base and 18in (46cm) high. However, you may find it easier to work the design in segments. When working a pattern in this way take care to align each piece of canvas with the centre front of the gown. The charts are marked with the vertical centres, and where spacing is important, I have included the bottom few stitches of the subsequent segment.

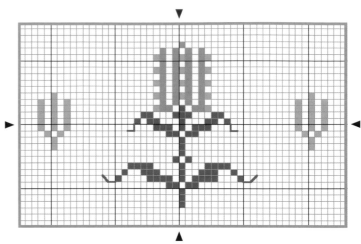

## You will need

Christening gown, plain white, with a yoke at least 2¼in (6cm) deep and a skirt approximately 25in (64cm) long.

14 count, waste canvas, 12 x 18in (20 x 45cm)

Tacking cotton

Stranded cotton: yellow, rose, pink, turquoise, green and dove grey

Sewing cotton and needle for oversewing and finishing

Tweezers

Masking tape

## Yoke

Embroider the yoke using a 2 x 2¾in (10 x 7cm) piece of waste canvas. If your gown fabric is fine, bind the spiky edges of the canvas with a narrow strip of masking tape. Centre the waste canvas over the area to be embroidered, matching the blue lines with the grain of the fabric, and tack it into position. Start the embroidery in the centre of the design, working the stitches through both fabrics using three strands of cotton, (two for very fine fabrics). Try not split the canvas threads. When the design is complete, remove the tacking threads and any masking tape. Dampen the canvas until it becomes limp and then, using tweezers, carefully dismantle the canvas thread by thread.

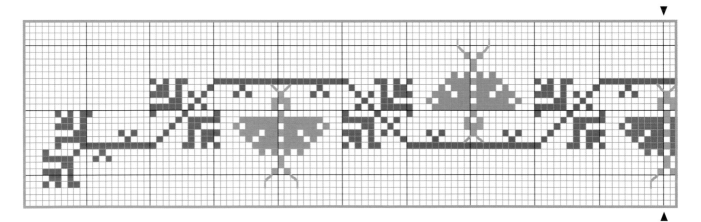

## Hem border

Secure a 15 x 2¼in (38 x 6cm) piece of waste canvas to the gown, work the design from the centre line outwards, then remove the canvas threads as described above.

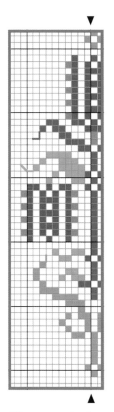

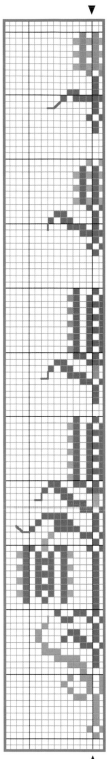

*Lower vertical segment*
Work the next part of the design, which includes the two doves and the three blue tulips, over an 8 x 5in (20 x 12.5cm) piece of waste canvas.

*Upper vertical segment*
In order to reproduce this segment of the pattern at the same scale as the others on these pages, it has been split into two parts. Work this segment of the design over a 3½ x 12¼in (9 x 31cm) piece of canvas.

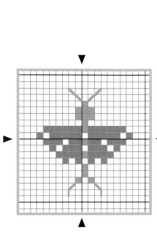

*Butterflies on the bias*
Finally work the two butterfly motifs over 2in (5cm) squares of waste canvas positioned on the bias.

When stitching is complete, and all the waste canvas removed, carefully press the gown from the wrong side on a very soft ironing cloth as described on page 13.

35

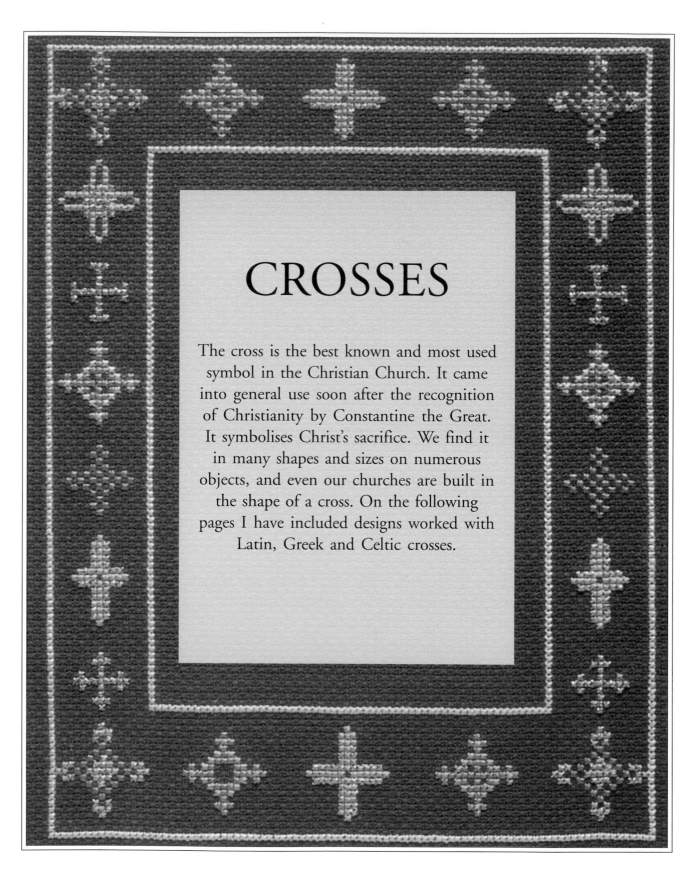

# CROSSES

The cross is the best known and most used symbol in the Christian Church. It came into general use soon after the recognition of Christianity by Constantine the Great. It symbolises Christ's sacrifice. We find it in many shapes and sizes on numerous objects, and even our churches are built in the shape of a cross. On the following pages I have included designs worked with Latin, Greek and Celtic crosses.

# Latin Cross

*The Latin cross is probably the most familiar of the Christian crosses. It has a long upright, the upper half of which is divided by a short horizontal bar.*

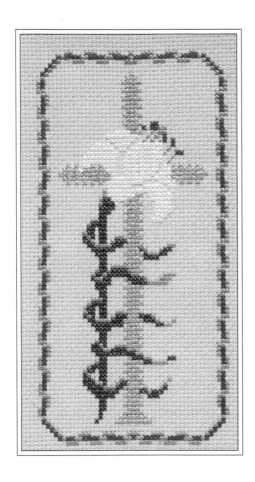

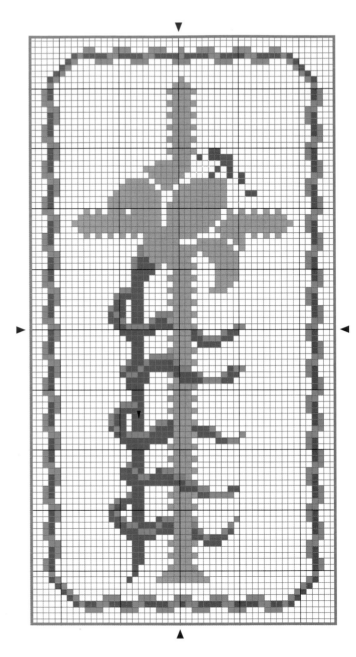

## Latin cross and lily panel

For this small panel a simple Latin cross is used with a lily which is featured on page 16. The motive is framed by a two coloured border.

---

*You will need:*

14 count, ecru, Aida Cloth, 8 x 12in (20 x 30cm)

Stranded cotton: light green, dark green, white, terracotta, yellow and gold.

Tapestry needle No. 24

---

Prepare the fabric and find the centre of the fabric as shown on page 12. Work the chart from the centre outwards, using two strands of cotton for the colours, but combine one strand of yellow and one strand of gold for the cross. Press the finished embroidery as described on page 13, and mount in a suitable picture frame.

# Greek Cross

*The Greek Cross also stands upright, but both segments of it are of equal length, which makes it a well-balanced square design.*

*This Greek cross was embroidered by Nina Mills. The gold metal frame round the lid is complemented by the small gold crosses within the main cross. A variation of this design is shown on page 48.*

## Box lid

The square shape of the Greek cross makes it an ideal decoration for the lid of a small square or circular box. The box shown here is typical of a wide range of 'blanks' that are available from craft suppliers. They can be finished with a cross-stitch embroidery or other forms of embellishment. The finished embroidery is laid into the metal frame of the lid, and held firmly in place by a metal disc that clips into place.

*You will need:*

Round ceramic box,
3in (7.5cm) diameter

14 count Aida cloth,
4in (10cm) square

Tapestry needle No. 26

Stranded cotton in pink, lilac, light green, mauve and gold

Prepare the fabric and find its centre as shown on page 12. Work the chart from the centre outwards using two strands of cotton.

Press your finished work as described on page 13, and then use sharp scissors, and the metal disc as a template, cut the fabric to size. Place the embroidery inside the lid and secure in place with the disc.

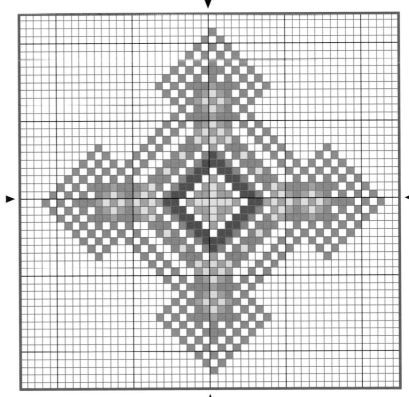

# Celtic Cross

*'Wheel-head' crosses were brought to the British Isles by Norsemen and were later adapted to Christianity. This form of cross was brought to England by Irish monks and is today known as a 'Celtic Cross'.*

*This Celtic cross prayer book cover and matching bookmark are embroidered in a restrained but very effective colour scheme.*

## Prayer book cover

Celtic crosses are often decorated with stylised beasts and human figures and with intricate knot patterns. I have used a stylised knot pattern in the design for this prayer book cover. The size of fabric shown below is for a book 8½ x 6in (21.5 x 15cm).

*You will need*

14 count, cream coloured Aida cloth, 9½ x 21¾in (24 x 55cm).

Lining fabric, the same size as the Aida cloth

Stranded cotton: navy and mid-blue

Tapestry needle No. 24 or 26

Needle and sewing cotton to match the colour of your fabric

Follow the instructions on pages 19–20 to find the starting point and to see how to make up the book cover. Use two strands of cotton for all stitches except for the background circle stitches, which need just one strand.

## Bookmark

The matching bookmark incorporates some of the elements of the Celtic cross design, to form a simple geometric pattern.

*You will need*

14 count, 2in (5cm) wide Aida band with a decorated edge, 9in (23cm) long

Stranded cotton: navy and mid blue

Tapestry needle No. 24 or 26

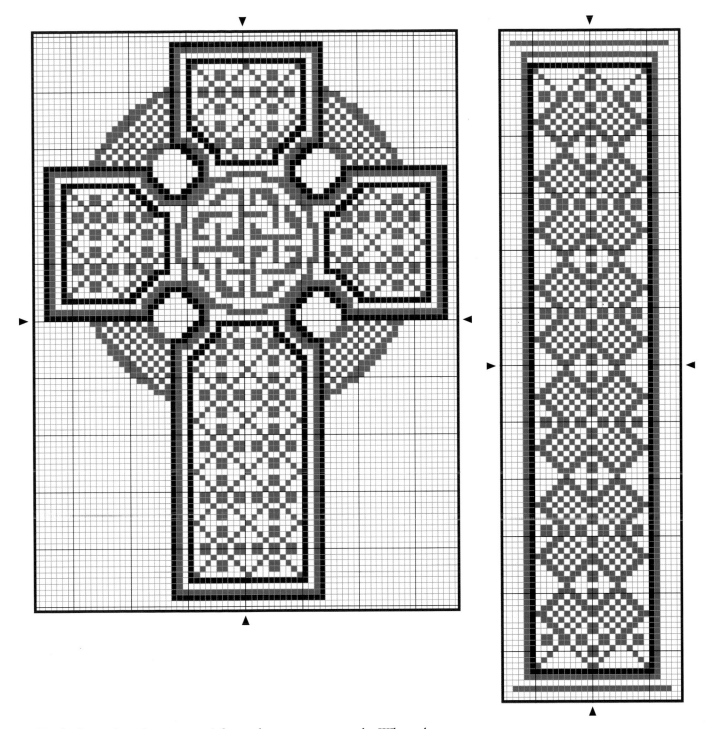

Work the embroidery as usual from the centre outwards. When the pattern is stitched, finish off with a row of tightly worked cross stitches across the full width of the band, approximately ¾in (2cm) from each cut end. Withdraw all weft threads beyond these rows of stitches to form fringes.

# BORDERS

Most motifs, especially small ones, look better when they are framed by a border, as this gives them some importance and stops them from getting lost in the background. Borders can also help unite a number of different motifs in a well-balanced design. Borders combined in a sampler can look very effective, as many examples from earlier centuries show. Some borders consist of continuous geometric patterns. However, any small motif or part of a design can be repeated or linked together to create a border.

A border should only enhance the design, not smother it. So, when choosing one, consider the size and colour of your design and try not to overpower it with a heavy or loudly coloured border.

*Borders are usually used in a supporting role (to frame or underline a motif) but a well-balanced arrangement of borders can make an attractive sampler, as well as a valuable memory aid for the embroiderer.*

43

# ALPHABETS

The geometric character of cross stitch makes it particularly suitable for many different types of lettering and numbers. Plain samplers and cards can be enriched with the addition of some text. Names and dates, for example, may be added to embroideries worked for a special person, or to commemorate a particular day.

Choose a style for your letters from the alphabet below – all capitals or initial capitals and lower case letters. Draw the text on to squared paper before embarking on the embroidery. Remember that individual letters must be spaced to form words and that words can be spaced to fit a design. Sort out the spacing for your text before you start your embroidery, to save any unnecessary unpicking. If the text extends to more than one line, make sure the spacing between the lines is pleasing to the eye and that the text forms a well-proportioned block.

*Some old alphabet samplers have become collectables. However, their original purpose, as examples of lettering for the composition of texts, should not be forgotten.*

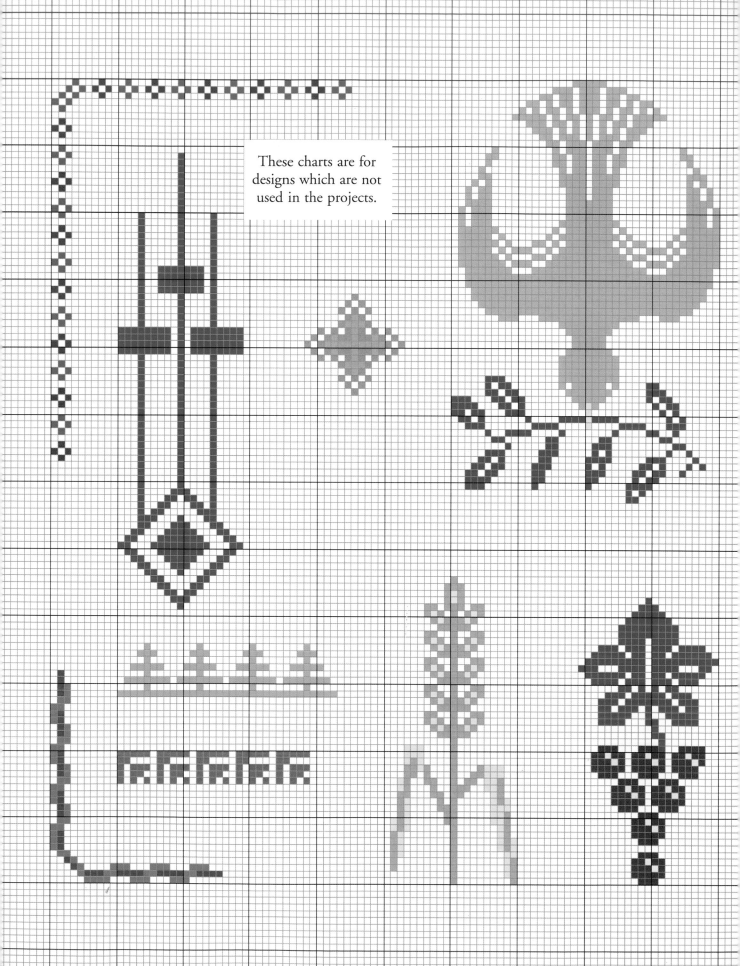

These charts are for designs which are not used in the projects.

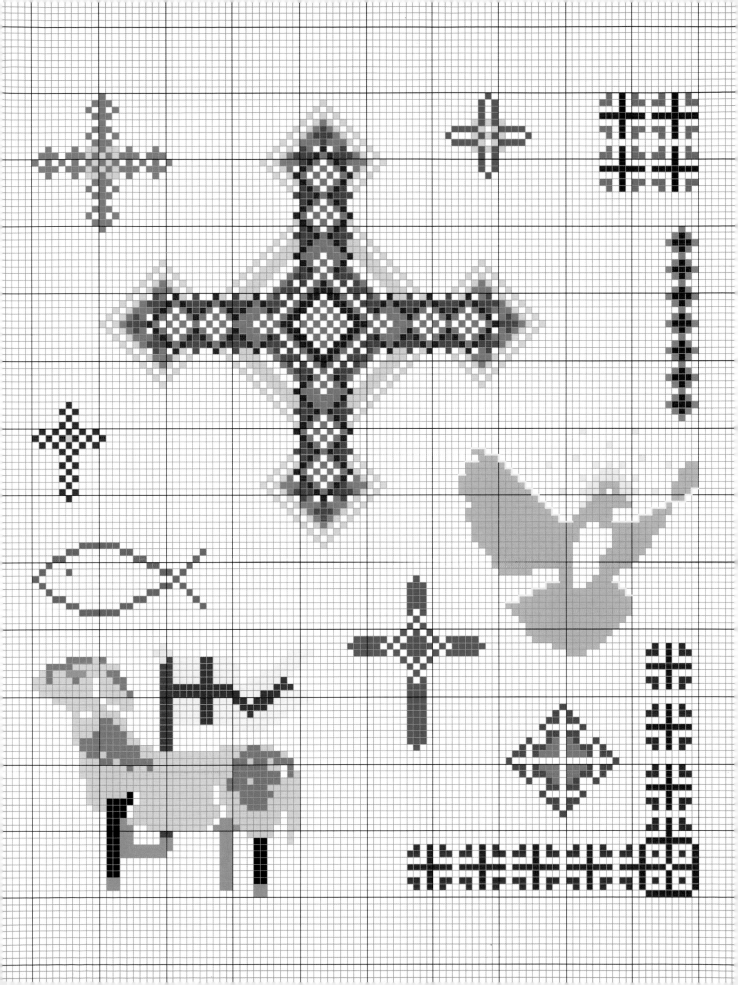

# INDEX

*A Greek cross worked on Aida cloth. The design consists of fifty-five stitches in both directions (see chart on page 47). Worked on 11 count Aida cloth or an 22 count evenweave fabric, the finished design would measure approximately 5in (13cm) square. Worked on 14 count Aida or 28 count evenweave it would measure approximately 4in (10cm).*